This Spine of Mine

Darbi McGee

Dedication

For my parents, brother, husband, and daughters, who have provided me with love, courage, strength, and support at every twist and turn throughout my life. Thank you for helping me find the beauty within and for always making me feel like I can do anything. I love you all.

About the Author

Darbi McGee was born with Lipomyelomeningocele, a form of Spina Bifida. At birth, her parents were told she might never walk or perform many daily activities independently. Despite enduring numerous surgeries and facing both physical and emotional challenges, Darbi has developed a sense of pride in her unique journey. She hopes her readers find themselves in her characters and draw strength from her stories, recognizing that their own experiences make them who they are.

Darbi holds a B.S. in Athletic Training and an M.A. in Teaching and Teacher Education. She is married with three daughters and runs a business specializing in handcrafted custom gifts and home décor. In addition, she teaches woodworking classes for youth.

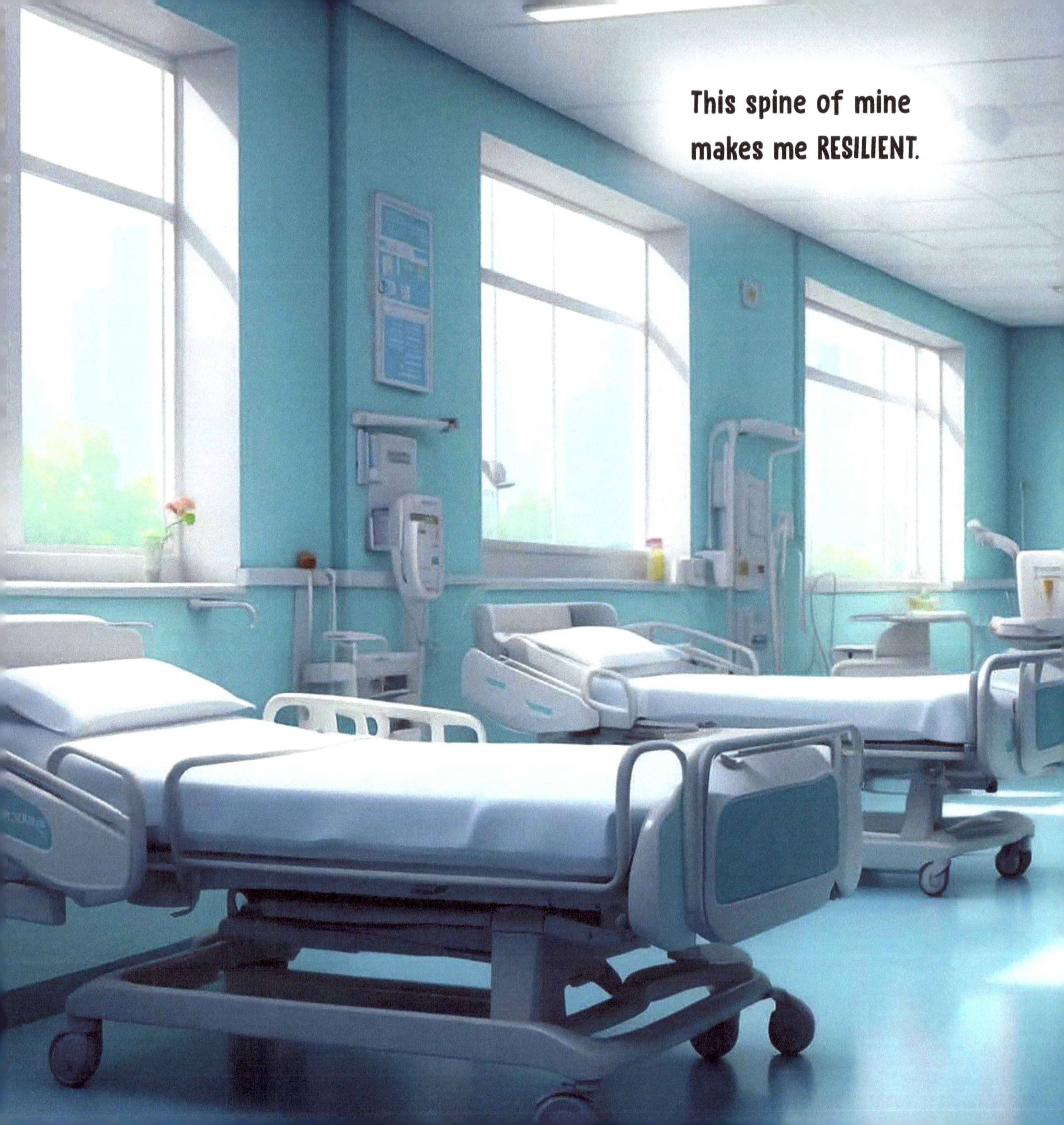

This spine of mine
makes me RESILIENT.

When I have surgery,
my mind learns to fight
just as hard as my body.

This spine of mine
makes me ADAPTABLE.

I see other kids walking, running, and jumping, and I learn to do it my own unique way.

This spine of mine
makes me COURAGEOUS.

I speak up for myself with my parents and doctors to ensure I get what I need to be successful.

This spine of mine
makes me EMPATHETIC.

I see that everyone faces different struggles and understand that they need kindness and encouragement.

This spine of mine
makes me DETERMINED.

Whether in school or physical therapy, I believe the only way to achieve a goal is by taking it one step at a time.

This spine of mine
makes me STRONG.

I know that any challenge that comes my way is simply another obstacle I can overcome.

This spine of mine
makes me GRATEFUL.

I am surrounded by loved ones
who always push me to be better
and lift me up when things
get hard.

This spine of mine
makes me INDEPENDENT.

Being encouraged to try things on
my own helps me to forge my own path.

This spine of mine
makes me OPTIMISTIC.

Even on my darkest days, I remain hopeful that I have the skills and abilities to make good things happen.

This spine of mine makes me DIFFERENT,
but it also makes me, ME!

And I couldn't be more
PROUD OF ME and YOU!